Contributors

Chindia Ilonka
Rox Burkey & Charles Breakfield
Tong Ge
Russell Little
Zane Carson Carruth
Candace MacPhie
Don Sawyer
J.M. Shaw
Jack E. Lewi, MD
JE Tarrow
Greg Dorchak
Mark Swaine
David Seaburn
Paul Harmon
Guy Quartley
Joe Abraham
L F Roth
Ruth C Mitchell
Fred Woodard
S.M. Stevens

Review Tales
A Book Magazine For Indie Authors

Founder & Editor in Chief: S. Jeyran Main
Publisher: Review Tales Publishing & Editing Services
Print & Distribution: Ingram Spark
Designs: Pexels
ISBN 978-1-988680-56-9 (Paperback)
ISBN 978-1-988680-57-6 (Digital)
www.jeyranmain.com
For all inquiries, please contact us directly.

Photo Credits from Pexels:
epta-studio-333887315-13929613
nati-87264186-20522243
eddson-lens-748406628-19100919.

Editor's Note

Hello Readers,

As we welcome you to the first issue of *Book Review Magazine*, we reflect on the journey that brought us here. Created as a space for indie authors to shine, this magazine celebrates their unique voices, diverse backgrounds, and unwavering commitment to storytelling. Each book featured in these pages is more than a work of fiction or memoir—it's a testament to the power of creativity and the resilience of the independent spirit. This collection showcases an elite selection of authors whose words will both captivate and inspire, hand-picked for their exceptional penmanship and distinctive narratives.

With a new year on the horizon, we look forward to the opportunities for the writing community. Independent authors profoundly shape the literary landscape, offering fresh perspectives, challenging norms, and connecting readers across cultures. As *Review Tales* grows, our mission remains steadfast: to provide a platform where these voices can be celebrated and their stories shared with readers who seek depth, originality, and authenticity.

In this issue, we're delighted to feature 20 carefully curated book reviews that spotlight the artistry and dedication of these incredible authors. Our wish for the coming year is to foster a community where stories and ideas flow freely and the beauty of independent writing is fully recognized. We hope these reviews ignite your passion for reading, encourage discovery, and perhaps even inspire your new works.

Here's to a year of powerful storytelling, boundless creativity, and the joy of the written word. Happy reading, and may 2025 be a year of endless literary journeys for us all.

Jeyran Main

Editor-in-Chief
Review Tales Magazine

WINTER 2025 | ISSUE 01

BOOK REVIEWS

Review Tales is thrilled to have reached the milestone of over 1,900 book reviews. With this extensive experience, we've had the privilege of exploring a vast range of literature. Our reviews are always impartial and thoughtfully crafted to highlight authors' strengths while inspiring them to keep creating. For this Winter issue, we've handpicked 20 exceptional book reviews to feature.

TO APPLY FOR A BOOK REVIEW VISIT WWW.JEYRANMAIN.COM

Book Reviews

- QUANTUM REBEL BY CHINDIA ILONKA
- TRUSTED FRIENDS AND LOVERS BY ROX BURKEY & CHARLES BREAKFIELD
- THE HOUSE FILLER BY TONG GE
- MURDER BY STORM BY RUSSELL LITTLE
- ABELLA AND THE ALMOST RACEHORSE BY ZANE CARSON CARRUTH
- FINDING COLOR BY CANDACE MACPHIE
- THE BURNING GEM BY DON SAWYER
- THE ASCENSION BY J.M. SHAW
- BE WELL BY JACK E. LEWI, MD
- THE TALLISTON CHRONICLES BY JE TARROW
- THEY AIN'T GONNA GET ANY DEADER BY GREG DORCHAK
- TALES FROM THE RED SUN VILLAGE VOL.2: THE X-RAY GLASSESBY MARK SWAINE
- UNTIL IT WAS GONE BY DAVID SEABURN
- SEVEN TREASURES BY PAUL HARMON
- DRAKOMUNDA BY GUY QUARTLEY
- KINGS, CONQUERORS, PSYCHOPATHS BY JOSEPH N ABRAHAM
- STARTING OVER BY L F ROTH
- JAXYL WARRIOR PRINCESS: A DARING ADVENTURE TALE OF LUST, LOVE AND DUTY BY RUTH C MITCHELL
- DEVELOPING YOUR SUPERNATURAL AWARENESSBY FRED WOODARD
- BEAUTIFUL AND TERRIBLE THINGS BY S.M. STEVENS

QUANTUM REBEL
Chindia Ilonka

Reviewer: Jeyran Main

Quantum Rebel by Chindia Ilonka is an inspiring and transformative guide for those seeking to elevate their leadership and life to a higher level of consciousness. The book is for business leaders and anyone ready to embrace a purpose-driven existence. Ilonka's powerful message encourages readers to move beyond traditional success, offering a compelling vision of what it means to live with deep inspiration and impact humanity at a transformative level.

Ilonka introduces the concept of "inner mastery"—a state of being where you are no longer just a "Work-in-Progress" but rather a "Work-in-Acceleration." This idea suggests that authentic leadership and success come from constant evolution, not just in external achievements but through the inner work of aligning with your soul's calling. This journey is about becoming a visionary leader who leads with clarity, inspiration, and authenticity, ultimately creating a ripple effect that inspires others to follow suit.

The book provides a blueprint for those ready to uncover their true potential as "Quantum Rebels"—visionary trailblazers who challenge the norms and work toward creating a world that benefits all. Ilonka's approach emphasizes that personal transformation is the key to collective change. As readers move through the pages, they are urged to ask themselves how to achieve success and fulfill their soul's purpose in a way that serves the greater good.

What makes *Quantum Rebel* stand out is its holistic approach. It encourages not just personal growth but social and environmental responsibility. The book blends spiritual awakening with actionable steps for leadership, making it both a philosophical and practical guide. Whether you're an entrepreneur, community leader, or someone on a personal growth journey, this book offers valuable insights on being an agent of positive, lasting change.

For anyone ready to transcend conventional limits and step into their most powerful, purposeful self, *Quantum Rebel* offers the tools, inspiration, and vision needed to lead from the soul and make a meaningful impact on the world.

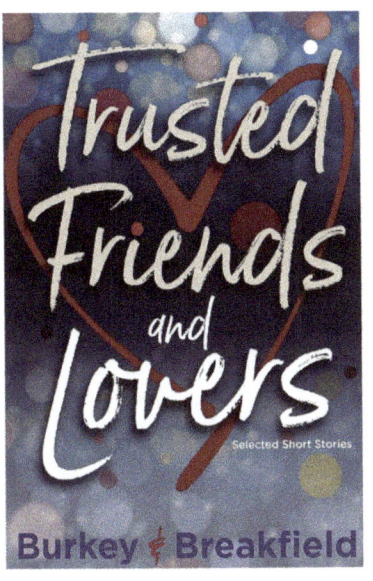

TRUSTED FRIENDS AND LOVERS
Rox Burkey & Charles Breakfield

Reviewer: Jeyran Main

In *Trusted Friends and Lovers*, authors Rox Burkey and Charles Breakfield explore the intricate dynamics of relationships through a series of compelling short stories. At the heart of these tales lies a question that resonates deeply with readers: What makes a person a trusted friend or lover, and how does it feel to have earned that status? Burkey and Breakfield invite readers to reflect on the fragile nature of trust and how it shapes the connections we form with others.

Each story in this collection delves into the emotional landscape of friendship and romance, focusing on the highs and lows that come with both. The authors skillfully portray the complexities of human relationships, where trust is often the glue that holds people together and the very thing that can unravel everything instantly. From the delicate moments of building trust to the devastating consequences when it is broken, *Trusted Friends and Lovers* captures its characters' emotional depth and vulnerability.

The stories range from heartwarming to heart-wrenching, offering readers a diverse exploration of relationships. Whether it's a steady, unwavering bond between old friends or lovers' passionate yet tumultuous journey, Burkey and Breakfield show that trust is not just a foundation—it's an ongoing process that requires effort, honesty, and vulnerability. The rocky roads these characters navigate are a testament to the challenges and rewards of building lasting connections.

This collection's ability to evoke empathy and understanding makes it stand out. The authors' writing and emotional insight allow readers to connect with the characters as their journeys reflect universal experiences of love, loss, and the pursuit of trust. The beauty of *Trusted Friends and Lovers* lies in its reminder that the journey is as important as the destination in any relationship. It also highlights how easily trust can be broken and how difficult it can be to rebuild once shattered.

In conclusion, *Trusted Friends and Lovers* is a thought-provoking collection that will resonate with anyone who has ever experienced the complexities of trust, love, and friendship. Through their engaging stories, Burkey and Breakfield invite readers to examine the bonds that define our lives and how we navigate the challenges that come with them.

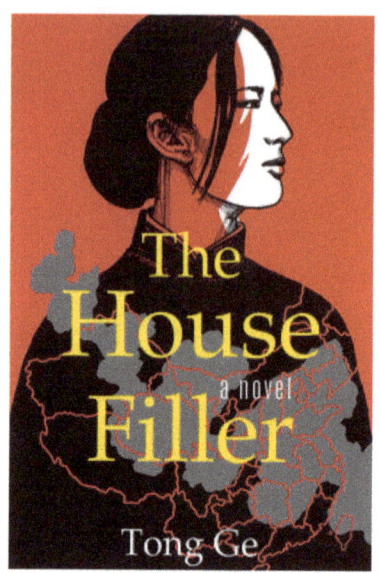

THE HOUSE FILLER
Tong Ge

Reviewer: Jeyran Main

The House Filler by Tong Ge takes readers on an emotional journey through one family's resilience in 20th-century China, a period marked by war, poverty, and political turmoil. Centered around Golden Phoenix, a strong and determined woman, the story captures her relentless fight to keep her family together as she faces one challenge after another.

Golden Phoenix's life unravels after her husband's sudden death, leaving her to raise her children in a country fractured by the Japanese invasion, civil war, and eventual Communist takeover. Struggling with poverty and desperation, she makes the heartbreaking choice to send her teenage twin sons to the Red Army, clinging to the hope of providing them with a better future. Her ordeal continues as she is forced to part with her two young daughters during the chaos of the Japanese occupation of her hometown. Meanwhile, her remaining son joins the Nationalist army, leaving Golden Phoenix and her adopted son to survive the brutal conditions of war-torn China.

The story climaxes as the civil war ends, and the Communist Party assumes power. One of Golden Phoenix's twins, now a Communist Party member, is unjustly accused of treason and sentenced to death. This devastating turn compels Golden Phoenix and her family to take desperate measures to save him, embodying her undying strength and devotion to her children.

Tong Ge's *The House Filler* profoundly explores the human spirit under extreme adversity. The author skillfully portrays Golden Phoenix's sacrifices, capturing the depth of a mother's love and resilience. Through vivid descriptions and historical detail, the novel immerses readers in the brutal reality of political oppression, illuminating the costs of ordinary families caught in sweeping historical currents.

With its compelling narrative and complex characters, *The House Filler* is a tribute to those who endured unimaginable hardships during China's tumultuous times. It's an unforgettable read for anyone interested in historical fiction that goes beyond the surface, presenting a powerful portrayal of survival, sacrifice, and love.

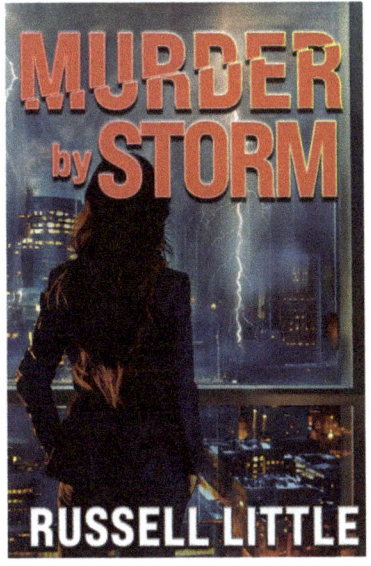

MURDER BY STORM
Russell Little

Reviewer: Jeyran Main

In *Murder By Storm*, Russell Little delivers a gripping and suspenseful crime thriller set against the backdrop of a hurricane ravaging Houston, Texas. The novel introduces Marilyn, a master of deception who has built a life of lies to protect her son while ensnaring innocent couples in her sinister schemes. Despite her violent and manipulative nature, Marilyn's ability to remain undetected makes her a compelling yet chilling character. However, the shadows of her past—particularly the haunting presence of her deranged mother and subservient stepfather—remain constant reminders of her troubled history.

On the other side of the battle is O.C. Simms, a disgraced detective obsessed with bringing Marilyn to justice. Fired for his inability to catch her after the mysterious death of her lover and lawyer, Ed, Simms refuses to let go of his belief that Marilyn is the mastermind behind his murder. Despite being stripped of his badge, Simms continues his vendetta against Marilyn, defying his former captain and relentlessly pursuing her through the streets of Houston.

As a catastrophic hurricane descends on the city, Marilyn sees both a threat and an opportunity. The storm's chaos provides the perfect cover for her to execute her most audacious plan yet, which could obliterate all evidence of her crimes and free her from justice. But Simms remains relentless, a determined force who will stop at nothing to catch her. The rising floodwaters create a high-stakes environment where both characters must fight for survival.

Murder By Story is a fast-paced, tension-filled thriller that keeps readers on the edge. Little expertly weaves together the elements of a stormy, chaotic setting with the cat-and-mouse pursuit between Marilyn and Simms, making this novel a thrilling ride from start to finish. With its intense action and morally complex characters, *Murder By Storm* is an engaging read for crime thriller enthusiasts who enjoy a high-stakes narrative and unpredictable twists.

ABELLA AND THE ALMOST RACEHORSE
Zane Carson Carruth

Reviewer: Jeyran Main

In *Abella and the Almost Racehorse*, Zane Carson Carruth brings young readers an enchanting story of friendship, perseverance, and dreams. The tale follows Abella, the World's First Tooth Fairy, and her friend Darcie as they encounter a horse aspiring to become a racehorse. However, this spirited horse faces a significant challenge—an aching tooth that keeps him from eating properly. Without the nourishment he needs, he worries he won't be able to grow strong enough to race.

This delightful story introduces children to themes of helping others, believing in dreams, and overcoming obstacles. The racehorse's journey captures the magic of ambition, showing that sometimes, it takes a little help from friends to bring dreams within reach. Abella, known for her magical abilities, quickly steps in to help. As the world's first Tooth Fairy, she's more than qualified to tackle the challenge of a toothache! With creativity and kindness, Abella helps the horse overcome his problem, allowing him to focus on his dream of becoming a champion.

The book offers readers a heartwarming look at friendship and support, demonstrating that even the smallest creatures, like a Tooth Fairy, can make a big difference. Carruth crafts a tale that resonates with young audiences through vibrant storytelling and relatable characters. Children will love following Abella's journey as she uses her magical talents to aid her friends, especially the determined racehorse who never gives up on his dream.

With themes of perseverance, kindness, and the power of friendship, *Abella and the Almost Racehorse* is a charming story that inspires children to pursue their goals, help others, and stay resilient in the face of challenges. Readers will be delighted as the racehorse finally meets his ideal trainer, realizing that with the proper support and determination, his dreams are closer than he ever imagined.

Carruth's story is engaging and teaches valuable life lessons, making *Abella and the Almost Racehorse* a memorable and inspiring addition to children's literature. This book will captivate young readers with its fantasy, fun, and cheerful messaging blend.

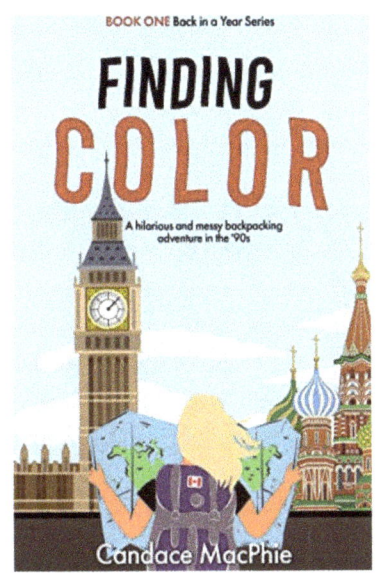

FINDING COLOR
Candace MacPhie

Reviewer: Jeyran Main

In *Finding Color*, Candace MacPhie delivers a charming and relatable journey of self-discovery, spiced with humor, heartache, and unexpected adventures. The protagonist, at twenty-five, feels trapped in a monotonous life following the death of her mother. Her routine consists of dull office meetings, lonely nights, and the kind of soul-crushing repetition that makes her feel decades older than her actual age. A life that once felt full of possibilities has been reduced to the dreariness of her current existence.

She seeks a fresh start and embarks on a life-changing three-week vacation to Greece, hoping to recapture a sense of adventure. There, she meets a man who sparks a renewed zest for life, and suddenly, her ordinary routine seems unbearable. After only a short time of rediscovering joy, she makes a bold decision—she sells everything she owns and heads for England, hoping to reunite with him and live a life far more vibrant than the one she's left behind.

However, life in London isn't the dream she imagined. Instead of a seamless transition to romance and excitement, she's confronted with the messiness of reality. She faces a roller-coaster relationship filled with misunderstandings, temp jobs, and quirky roommates, including Aussies, Kiwis, and a scandalous Spanish couple. The dream she thought would be easy turns into a whirlwind of complications, yet she begins to understand that the fulfillment she's searching for is not an escape from life's problems but a confrontation with them.

MacPhie's writing is witty and warm, with the protagonist's personal growth unfolding in a way that feels both realistic and deeply satisfying. Her journey is filled with deliciously awkward and often cringeworthy moments, making her struggle entertaining and relatable. *Finding Color* is a reminder that life's most meaningful moments come not from running away but from facing the unexpected and that true happiness lies in embracing life's imperfections.

With its engaging narrative, vivid characters, and uplifting message, this novel will resonate with anyone who's ever dreamed of breaking free and finding a life more vibrant than the one they know.

THE BURNING GEM
Don Sawyer

Reviewer: Jeyran Main

In *The Burning Gem*, Don Sawyer takes readers on a thrilling, mystical journey that blends adventure, intrigue, and the supernatural. At its heart, the novel is a story of transformation, danger, and the pursuit of truth, all set against the backdrop of a hidden world where souls are captured and turned into precious jewels.

The protagonist, Barbara, is a woman trapped in a loveless marriage, yearning for something more. Her life turns unexpectedly when she encounters Zoltan, a mysterious artisan who crafts gems imbued with souls. After an encounter with him, part of Barbara's soul is crystallized into a blazing red gem, awakening her dormant empathic abilities. Seeking a way to reconnect with Zoltan and escape her soul-crushing life, Barbara embarks on a perilous journey through the dark and dangerous New York subway tunnels, determined to uncover the secrets of the gem and the man who created it.

Zoltan, a 110-year-old gem maker, leads a life of opulent bitterness, bound by a contract with the Mester—a sinister figure who controls the dark forces behind the gem-making enterprise. Zoltan's life is filled with secrecy and forbidden rules, but his curiosity and growing unease lead him to question the true nature of his work and the twisted world he inhabits.

The novel's plot escalates as Barbara and Zoltan delve deeper into the dark underworld of seers, shapeshifters, and ancient knowledge, with the stakes rising as they uncover the sinister truth behind the Market and the Mester's deadly plans. From the forgotten subway station in New York to the ruined bars and dark alleys of Budapest, their journey is a desperate race to prevent a catastrophe that could alter the fate of their world.

Sawyer's storytelling is rich with atmosphere, filled with mystery and tension that keeps readers engaged from start to finish. *The Burning Gem* is a fascinating blend of supernatural intrigue and dark adventure, offering a unique take on soul-searching and the hidden forces that shape our lives. With well-drawn characters and a plot full of twists, this novel will captivate fans of fantasy and thrillers, leaving them eager to discover what lies beyond the gem.

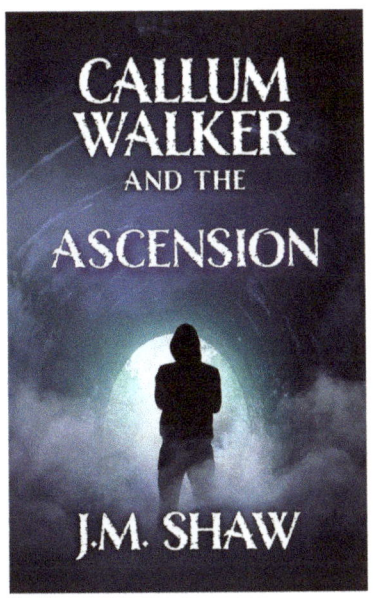

THE ASCENSION
J.M. Shaw

Reviewer: Jeyran Main

The Ascension by J.M. Shaw introduces readers to a thrilling world of magic, warfare, and destiny. In this fast-paced fantasy novel, Shaw blends the supernatural with the every day as two brothers—one a sorcerer and the other a necromancer—wage a hidden war that threatens both the magical and natural worlds. As these formidable enemies marshal mythical creatures and deadly forces, their battle for supremacy could forever alter the balance of reality.

Callum Walker is, at the story's heart, an introverted young man struggling to understand his mysterious gifts. When monstrous creatures begin terrorizing his city, Callum is reluctantly thrust into action. He must learn to harness his unrefined arcane powers to fight back, even as the two warring brothers, each with their agenda, take notice of his growing abilities and see him as a potential threat.

As Callum grapples with his newfound powers, he uncovers an ancient prophecy that links him to the ongoing conflict. It is foretold that he will be the one to end the war between the sorcerer and necromancer, but Callum soon realizes that his path to fulfilling this destiny will be perilous. Not only must he confront the agents of both factions who relentlessly pursue him, but he must also navigate a world that is increasingly foreign and dangerous.

Shaw's world-building is rich and immersive, drawing readers into a world where magic exists beyond human perception, veiled in secrecy. The suspense builds as Callum learns more about the prophecy and his role in it, pushing him to face his fears and doubts about whether he is to survive —and, perhaps, to end the destructive war raging behind the veil.

The Ascension is an engaging blend of action, mystery, and fantasy, with solid character development and a gripping plot that will captivate fans of magical warfare and epic quests. Shaw delivers an exciting start to what promises to be an unforgettable series, leaving readers eagerly awaiting what will come next.

BE WELL
Jack E. Lewi, MD

Reviewer: Jeyran Main

Dr. Jack E. Lewi invites readers to explore wellness and self-discovery in Be Well. As a physician and retired U.S. Army Colonel, Lewi brings a unique perspective to the concept of health, integrating holistic principles with insights drawn from his extensive experience in medicine. This Kindle edition is more than just a book; it is a heartfelt collection of quotes and poems that serve as soulful reflections, inspiring readers to seek peace, love, joy, and overall wellness.

The power of words resonates throughout *Be Well*, as Lewi curates diverse literature that has influenced his understanding of wellness. Each quote and poem acts as a stepping stone, guiding readers to contemplate their paths of thinking and fulfillment. The collection reflects Lewi's deep appreciation for the transformative nature of language, demonstrating how the right words can motivate and uplift us in times of need.

Dr. Lewi's holistic approach is evident in his exploration of wellness, which encompasses physical, mental, and spiritual well-being. His passion for running, fitness, nutrition, and meditation shines through, providing a well-rounded perspective on being well. The integration of Eastern and Western philosophies adds depth to his reflections, allowing readers to consider a variety of viewpoints on health and healing.

What sets *Be Well* apart is its accessibility. The concise format and carefully selected quotes make it easy for readers to engage with the material at their own pace. Whether you're seeking motivation for your wellness journey or simply looking for moments of inspiration throughout your day, this book is a valuable resource.

In conclusion, *Be Well* is a beautifully crafted compilation that encapsulates the essence of wellness through the wisdom of others. Jack E. Lewi, MD, has created a nurturing space for readers to explore their journeyward health and happiness. This book is a must-read for anyone interested in holistic wellness and the profound impact of words on our lives. Enjoy, heal, and embrace the journey to be well.

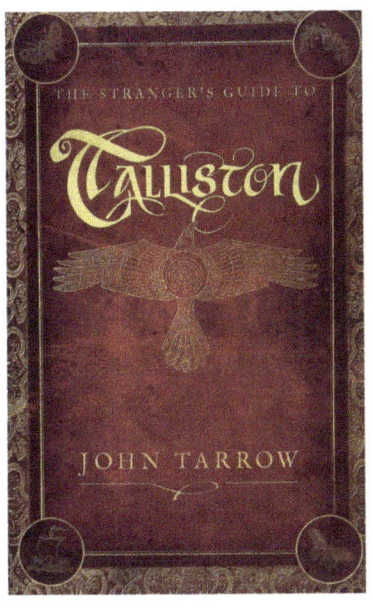

THE STRANGER'S GUIDE TO TALLISTON
John Tarrow

Reviewer: Jeyran Main

The Stranger's Guide To Talliston by John Tarrow is an enchanting young adult fantasy adventure that transports readers to the heart of Britain's most extraordinary home: Talliston House & Gardens. With a captivating premise and a richly imagined world, Tarrow's debut novel weaves a tale of magic, mystery, and the quest for belonging.

The story follows thirteen-year-old Joe, whose life takes a dramatic turn when he stumbles into an abandoned council house, only to find himself ensnared within a labyrinth that guards the last magical places on Earth. Tarrow masterfully constructs this maze as a physical and metaphorical journey for Joe as he navigates through a series of dark and treacherous rooms. The labyrinth serves as a poignant backdrop, symbolizing Joe's struggles with isolation and the search for his missing parents.

At the labyrinth's heart lies *The Stranger's Guide*, a cryptic book that becomes Joe's lifeline and maps through this perilous world. Tarrow's imaginative storytelling shines as he crafts a narrative filled with suspense and intrigue, drawing readers deeper into the labyrinthine mystery. Joe's encounters with sinister forces add an element of danger, keeping readers on the edge of their seats as he unravels the secrets hidden within Talliston.

What sets this novel apart is its inspiration rooted in the real-life transformation of Talliston House. The author's meticulous attention to detail brings the extraordinary home to life, making it a character in its own right. Tarrow's vivid descriptions allow readers to experience the wonder and magic of this unique space, enhancing the overall immersion in the story.

The Stranger's Guide To Talliston is more than just a fantasy adventure; it is a heartfelt exploration of family, courage, and the resilience of the human spirit. Joe's journey is relatable, resonating with anyone who has ever felt lost or disconnected. Tarrow's deft blend of fantasy and reality creates a rich tapestry that will appeal to readers of all ages.

In conclusion, John Tarrow has crafted a compelling debut that captures the imagination and invites readers into a world of wonder and discovery.

THEY AIN'T GONNA GET ANY DEADER
Greg Dorchak

Reviewer: Jeyran Main

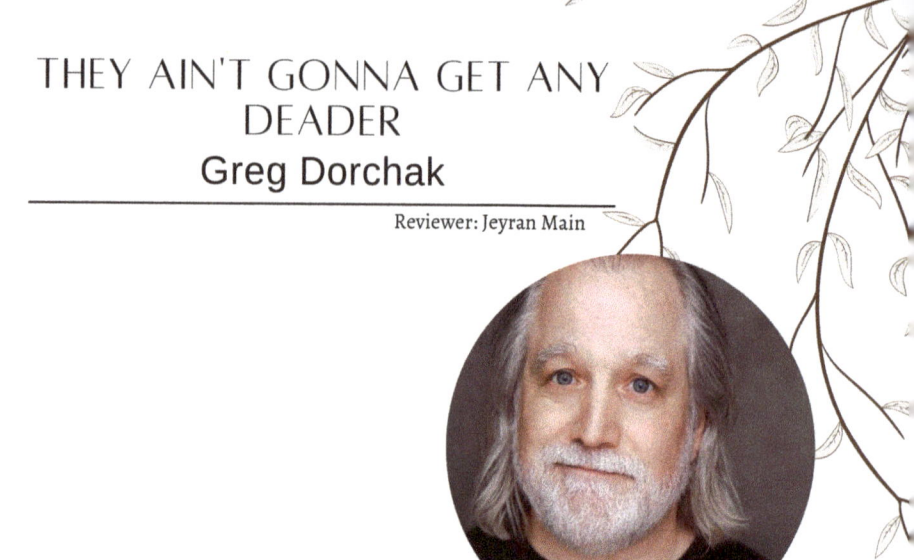

In *They Ain't Gonna Get Any Deader*, Greg Dorchak presents a witty collection of personal essays that encapsulate the trials of adolescence. As his eighth book and second essay collection, Dorchak invites readers to journey through his high school and college years, showcasing his signature humor, introspection, and sharp wit.

Dorchak's storytelling is vivid and relatable, depicting the awkward yet exhilarating moments that define coming-of-age. Each essay is infused with a playful irreverence, drawing readers into the often hilarious realities of youth. Whether recounting the challenges of navigating friendships, academics, or young love, Dorchak's ability to find humor in the mundane makes his essays entertaining and thought-provoking.

What sets this collection apart is Dorchak's introspective approach. He reflects on the lessons learned during his formative years, offering a glimpse into the mindset of a young adult grappling with identity and self-discovery. His candid anecdotes resonate with anyone who has experienced the awkwardness of adolescence, making his reflections feel personal yet universal.

Dorchak's humor is a unifying thread, transforming cringe-worthy moments into opportunities for laughter. His knack for storytelling ensures that readers are not just passive observers but active participants in his shared journey. The essays are crafted with a keen eye for detail, revisiting the past with nostalgia and a humorous twist.

In conclusion, *They Ain't Gonna Get Any Deader* is a delightful read that will resonate with anyone who has navigated the choppy waters of youth. Greg Dorchak's humor and introspection make this collection a refreshing exploration of coming-of-age, reminding us that laughter can be the best remedy, even in our most challenging moments. This book is a testament to the enduring power of storytelling, leaving readers chuckling long after the last page is turned.

TALES FROM THE RED SUN VILLAGE VOL.2
Mark Swaine

Reviewer: Jeyran Main

Tales from the Red Sun Village Vol. 2 by Mark Swaine presents a narrative that explores themes of desperation, power, and the consequences of revenge. The story follows a teenage boy named Juan, his older sister Martina, and their friend Leo, fleeing from a local cartel in Mexico due to an unpaid debt.

The plot begins with the trio considering theft as a means of survival. They target Tucker, a reclusive American who was a client of their late grandmother, Marianna, a dedicated cleaner. Unbeknownst to them, Tucker is a retired CIA agent with a pair of x-ray glasses. These glasses have significant capabilities, allowing the user to see through objects and manipulate time, space, and matter.

Upon realizing the gravity of the situation, Tucker, who is dealing with grief from Marianna's passing, chooses to assist Juan and his friends. He provides them with the X-ray glasses to combat the cartel that threatens their lives. This decision propels Juan into a series of fantastical adventures, including time travel to the Cretaceous Period and encounters with alien worlds. Throughout these experiences, Juan grapples with the immense power of the glasses, which fuels his desire for vengeance against the cartel members.

As the narrative progresses, a central theme emerges regarding the nature of power. Juan's increasing obsession with using the glasses leads him down a dangerous path, demonstrating the adage that absolute power corrupts absolutely. The story culminates in a conflict where Juan's friends must intervene to prevent him from unleashing catastrophic consequences driven by his thirst for revenge.

Mark Swaine's *The X-Ray Glasses* effectively combines adventure and moral reflection elements, making it a relevant addition to contemporary young adult literature. The book addresses critical issues such as the implications of violence, the complexities of grief, and the ethical considerations surrounding power and its use. The narrative structure, character development, and thematic depth contribute to its potential impact on readers, particularly those interested in the intersections of personal struggle and fantastical elements.

UNTIL IT WAS GONE
David B. Seaburn

Reviewer: Jeyran Main

David B. Seaburn's *Until It Was Gone* is a poignant exploration of love, loss, and the struggle for connection within a fractured family. The novel opens dramatically with Laney's shocking announcement at their fortieth-anniversary dinner: she is leaving Franklin. This revelation sends Franklin into a spiral of confusion and heartache as he questions the love that once defined their marriage. Laney's response, "Yes, until it was gone," encapsulates the book's central theme—how love can fade under the pressures of life and unresolved issues.

Laney's journey to the Oklahoma panhandle in search of their estranged daughter Roz, who left home at sixteen, adds layers to the narrative. As she seeks to reconnect with Roz and meet her granddaughter Maggie for the first time, the story delves into the complexities of familial bonds and the yearning for reconciliation. Meanwhile, Franklin grapples with the physical and emotional ramifications of contracting COVID, which evolves into long-term COVID-19, forcing him to confront painful memories of abuse from his father. This dual narrative beautifully illustrates how the past can haunt us, shaping our present unexpectedly.

As the story unfolds, Seaburn introduces additional layers of tension with Maggie's unexpected pregnancy and the dire need for an abortion in a state where it is outlawed. The stakes escalate, compelling the characters to navigate their fears and desires while striving to support one another. The juxtaposition of personal struggles against the backdrop of contemporary societal challenges resonates deeply, reflecting the harsh realities many families face today.

Until It Was Gone celebrates resilience, hope, and the fragile threads that connect us. Seaburn's sensitive portrayal of his characters invites readers to reflect on their relationships and the importance of holding onto hope, even in the darkest times. This novel is a compelling reminder that, despite the turmoil, the desire for connection and understanding can lead us toward healing and redemption.

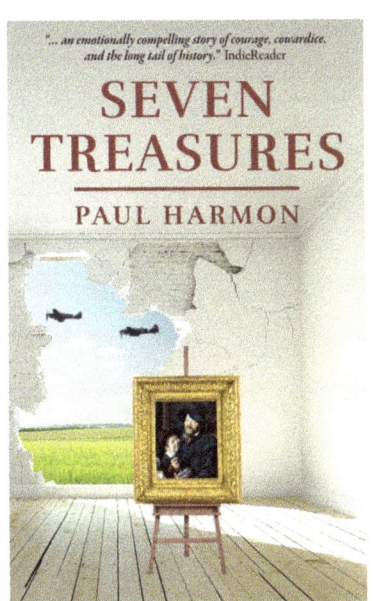

SEVEN TREASURES
Paul Harmon

Reviewer: Jeyran Main

In *Seven Treasures*, Paul Harmon weaves a captivating tale that bridges past and present, blending mystery, art, love, and the haunting shadows of war. Set in the enchanting French village of Villemont, the story follows Mark, an Australian man adrift after a divorce and career loss, who impulsively buys a house in France. Arriving with little more than hopes of reinvention, he begins to sell items from his attic, unaware that some of the dusty bric-a-brac are priceless treasures once coveted by Nazi commander Hermann Goering.

Harmon expertly unfolds the mystery when Mark and Monique, his newfound love, begin restoring an unassuming painting left unsold at the market. They soon suspect it might be a 16th-century Dutch masterpiece, and their search for its provenance reveals a dark, complex history that changes their lives. This discovery links them to a powerful legacy of betrayal and redemption, bringing the village's hidden wartime sins into the light.

Interwoven with Mark's story is the harrowing 1941 narrative of Josef, a young anti-fascist art student coerced into Goering's art-looting unit in Nazi-occupied Paris. Josef's silent rebellion against the Nazi regime and his risky decision to aid a Jewish woman fleeing with her family's precious artwork create a powerful storyline of courage. Harmon's portrayal of Josef's moral struggle profoundly affects him, capturing the desperation of those caught in the crossfire of war and their forced choices.

The novel's dual timelines work seamlessly, contrasting Mark's journey of self-discovery with Josef's wartime experiences. Harmon crafts a layered and atmospheric story that immerses readers in the mysteries of art history and the powerful, often painful, legacies we inherit. For Kate Morton and Kristin Harmel fans, *Seven Treasures* delivers intrigue and emotional depth, exploring how the echoes of love, war, and art can resonate across decades.

Ultimately, *Seven Treasures* is a richly textured story about finding redemption amidst the ruins of history and discovering hope where it's least expected. Harmon's narrative reminds us that even the darkest secrets can lead to light and that every mystery holds the potential for transformation.

DRAKOMUNDA
Guy Quartley

Reviewer: Jeyran Main

In *Drakomunda*, Guy Quartley invites readers into a dark fantasy world where magic and horror intertwine to create an epic tapestry of interwoven lives and mystical forces. Over millennia, the fates of various characters converge, each influenced by the clash between the malevolent energy of a poisonous star and the serpentine soul of the Earth. This collision of powers sets the stage for a gripping narrative that explores the depths of human experience against a backdrop of supernatural intrigue.

Quartley's storytelling is rich and immersive, drawing readers into a universe that pulsates with life, danger, and a palpable sense of foreboding. The author's ability to craft vivid landscapes and intricate character arcs enhances the sense of scale and complexity, making it easy to become engrossed in the unfolding drama. Each character is carefully developed, their motivations and struggles intricately tied to the more significant cosmic conflict, which adds layers of depth to the narrative.

The themes of interconnection and the consequences of choices resonate throughout *Drakomunda*. As characters navigate their paths, they are often faced with moral dilemmas that reflect the chaotic nature of their world. The poisonous star symbolizes destructive power, while the Earth's serpentine soul represents resilience and wisdom, creating a compelling duality that permeates the story. Quartley deftly explores how these forces shape not only the characters' destinies but also the fabric of the world itself.

The blending of dark fantasy elements with horror creates an atmosphere that is both thrilling and unsettling. Quartley does not shy away from exploring the darker aspects of the human experience, making for a narrative as thought-provoking as it is entertaining. The tension builds steadily, leading to climactic moments that keep readers on the edge of their seats.

In conclusion, *Drakomunda* is a captivating read that skillfully merges fantasy, magic, and horror into a powerful narrative about interconnected lives and the forces that shape them. Guy Quartley's masterful storytelling and rich world-building will appeal to fans of dark fantasy looking for a thought-provoking exploration of the complexities of existence. This book is a must-read for anyone who revels in tales that challenge perceptions and delve into the unknown.

KINGS, CONQUERORS PSYCH PATHS

From Alexander to Hitler
to the Corporation

KINGS, CONQUERORS, PSYCHOPATHS FROM ALEXANDER TO HITLER TO THE CORPORATION
Joseph N. Abraham MD

Reviewer: Jeyran Main

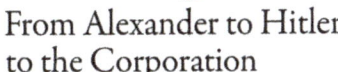

JOSEPH N. ABRAHAM, MD

In *Kings, Conquerors, Psychopaths*, Joseph N. Abraham, MD, sheds light on the grim origins of civilization, proposing that power has always been built upon violence, manipulation, and tyranny. Abraham provocatively argues that conquest is nothing more than "murder and theft," that kings and conquerors were essentially "vicious criminals," and that these criminals shaped the world in which we now live. He dismantles the romanticized view of monarchs as wise and just, portraying them instead as some of the "most vicious psychopaths, narcissists, and sadists" in history. Their brutal legacy is evident even in today's political and corporate worlds.

Abraham goes further, likening modern corporations to ancient empires, suggesting that they have inherited many of the same oppressive tactics once employed by historical tyrants. He contends that money has become the weapon of choice today. Through financial and corporate power, oppression persists, enforcing compliance and shaping society's values, just as emperors once commanded absolute obedience. His perspective suggests that our liberty is fragile, an illusion sustained by systems designed to control it.

One of the most compelling aspects of Abraham's work is his discussion of contemporary authoritarianism. He argues that our focus should not be solely on the leaders themselves but also on the unthinking loyalty of their followers. Without this blind support, he claims, despots would be powerless. This insight challenges readers to question why societies gravitate toward authoritarian figures and continue to defend even their hypocrisies.

This book, well-written and meticulously researched, is both provocative and haunting. It invites readers to confront the uncomfortable truth that civilization, past and present, is built on a foundation of control and subjugation. For those interested in politics, history, or sociology, *Kings, Conquerors, and Psychopaths* offer a fresh lens on the past and an ominous reflection on the present. Abraham's insight into the resilience of oppressive power structures will resonate with those willing to read with an open mind and acknowledge that while the faces of tyranny may have changed, the structures that empower them endure.

STARTING OVER
L. F. Roth

Reviewer: Jeyran Main

Set against the evocative backdrop of an English boarding school in 1966, *Starting Over* by L. F. Roth invites readers to embark on a transformative journey. This captivating tale introduces a diverse cast of characters, each navigating complexities while working with children with unique abilities. The narrative unfolds in a world that resonates with students' and mentors' dreams, aspirations, and challenges.

Roth expertly weaves a tapestry of relationships, depicting how the characters' needs intertwine. The boarding school serves as a microcosm of society, where vulnerability becomes a source of strength. As educators and students interact, they forge unexpected alliances, highlighting the profound impact of empathy and understanding. The characters are beautifully fleshed out, each contributing to a more significant personal growth and resilience narrative.

Throughout the story, the winds of change blow through the halls of the school, prompting characters to confront the discomfort of the unknown. Roth deftly captures the essence of transformation, illustrating how individuals can evolve when faced with trials. The narrative resonates with the reader, reminding us to embrace change and seek solace in shared experiences.

As the characters navigate their challenges, *Starting Over* explores themes of personal growth, resilience, and the transformative power of human connection. *Starting Over* is poignant and reflective, allowing readers to engage deeply with the character's landscape. The story reminds us that we can find strength and support in unexpected places through shared vulnerabilities.

In conclusion, *Starting Over* is a beautifully crafted tale with rich character development and exploration of human relationships. This book encourages readers to reflect on their journeys and the potential for new beginnings, making this a compelling read for anyone seeking inspiration and insight into the complexities of life.

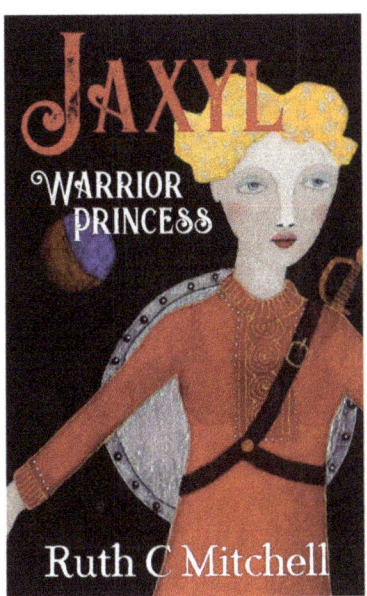

JAXYL WARRIOR PRINCESS
Ruth C. Mitchell

Reviewer: Jeyran Main

In *Jaxyl Warrior Princess*, Ruth C. Mitchell invites readers into a vibrant and imaginative world filled with adventure, romance, and a strong feminist perspective. This second volume of the Karda saga centers on Jaxyl, a fierce warrior princess navigating the challenges of love and duty as she raises her messianic daughter, Yez. With its fast-paced narrative, the novel promises a thrilling journey from start to finish.

Mitchell's writing captivates from the very first page, immersing readers in the richly crafted universe of Merth. The storyline weaves together riveting love scenes and triumphant battles, showcasing Jaxyl's dynamic character and unapologetic approach to life. As one critic aptly says, "You will never know anyone as exciting as the great Jaxyl Warrior Princess." This sentiment encapsulates the essence of Jaxyl—she is daring, rebellious, and refreshingly complex, embodying the qualities of a heroine who resonates with modern readers.

The book shines not only in its action-packed plot but also in its linguistic creativity. Mitchell introduces strange languages and cultural nuances that enrich the reading experience, making the world of Merth feel unique and immersive. Critics have praised the book for its well-crafted storyline and professional editing, emphasizing its appeal to fans of character-driven narratives and space battles.

Reviewers have noted that *Jaxyl Warrior Princess* is more than just an adventure tale; it celebrates female empowerment and individuality. Jaxyl's choices may be bold and controversial, but they reflect her determination to carve her own in a universe of obstacles. This feminist adventure romance captivates readers not only through its thrilling plot but also by challenging traditional norms and expectations.

Jaxyl Warrior Princess is a must-read for those seeking an engaging story that combines action, romance, and a strong female lead. Ruth C. Mitchell's talent for storytelling shines through in this compelling tale, making it a worthy addition to the genre and a delight for readers of all ages.

DEVELOPING YOUR SUPERNATURAL AWARENESS
Dr. Fredrick Woodard

Reviewer: Jeyran Main

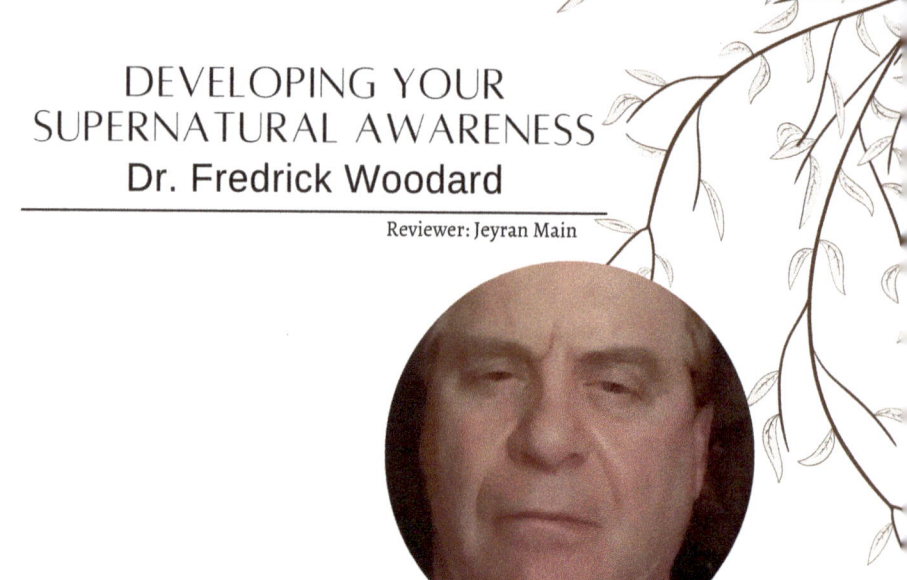

In *Developing Your Supernatural Awareness*, the author begins an introspective journey exploring the often-overlooked realm of supernatural experiences. The book serves as both a personal narrative and a guide, prompting readers to consider their interactions with the unseen forces shaping our lives.

The author candidly shares their history with supernatural events, providing a rich tapestry of experiences ranging from early encounters with hypnosis to profound studies of consciousness. These reflections illuminate the author's evolution as a professional and shed light on how such experiences can deepen our understanding of ourselves and our place in the universe. Including critical figures who influenced the author's path adds depth to the narrative, illustrating how relationships can guide our exploration of the supernatural.

One of the book's strengths is its ability to bridge personal anecdotes with broader philosophical concepts. The author discusses how they improved their understanding of supernatural awareness, emphasizing the importance of connecting with an interactive universe filled with invisible beings, energies, and information. This perspective challenges readers to think beyond the material world and consider the profound ways in which we can interact with the universe around us.

The writing is engaging and thought-provoking, inviting readers to embark on their explorations of the supernatural. The author's insights encourage us to question our perceptions and embrace the mysteries of existence. As we navigate the pages, we are reminded that the universe is not a static entity but a dynamic force that can enhance our understanding of reality.

In conclusion, *Developing Your Supernatural Awareness* is a compelling read for anyone interested in the intersections of consciousness, spirituality, and personal growth. It invites us to explore the unseen aspects of our lives, encouraging readers to cultivate their supernatural awareness and connect with the interactive universe surrounding us. Whether you are a seasoned practitioner or a curious newcomer, this book offers valuable insights into the limitless possibilities of the supernatural.

BEAUTIFUL AND TERRIBLE THINGS
S.M. Stevens

Reviewer: Jeyran Main

In *Beautiful and Terrible Things*, S.M. Stevens presents a nuanced portrait of life in a modern city where cultural vibrancy meets the stark realities of social issues. Released by Black Rose Writing, this novel captures the essence of urban existence, weaving themes of friendship, personal validation, and transformation amid the chaos of contemporary society.

Set against a diverse and dynamic cityscape, Stevens unfolds a tapestry of interconnected lives, illustrating how human connections shape, uplift, and sometimes fracture the lives they touch. Through her characters' experiences, readers are led to reflect on the profound influence of friendship, the challenges inherent in authentic connections, and the complexity of personal transformation. These elements make the narrative both enlightening and deeply relatable, inviting readers to ponder the dynamics of their relationships.

The book has earned high praise, receiving multiple 5-star reviews and acclaim from literary communities. It was named a Finalist in the General Fiction category of the American Fiction Awards. It earned an Honorable Mention in the Fiction - Social Issues category of the Readers' Favorite International Book Award Contest. These accolades underscore the novel's resonant themes and Stevens' ability to engage readers on multiple levels, tackling life's beautiful and painful aspects.

Stevens' writing is poignant yet accessible, skillfully pulling readers into the lives and emotions of her characters. She explores the balance of joyful, celebratory moments with painful, often silent struggles, reflecting the duality of life and how joy and hardship frequently coalesce. This harmony within the narrative fosters an impactful and memorable story, drawing readers into a rich, realistic portrayal of human interaction and growth.

Ultimately, *Beautiful and Terrible Things* offers a thought-provoking exploration of urban life, making it an engaging and resonant addition to contemporary fiction. S.M. Stevens has crafted a compelling story highlighting friendship's challenges and triumphs in an ever-evolving world. This novel serves as a testament to the resilience and transformative power of relationships, making it a must-read for those interested in exploring the depths of human connection within the complexities of today's society.